I AM Empowered

A COLLECTION OF WORDS THAT EMPOWER, ENLIGHTEN, AND SUPPORT YOUR FULL BEING.

BY: TIFFANY WRIGHT, MSW

ISBN: 979-8-2180-9357-0

Contents

Introduction

Words have the power to transform your mind. Words have the power to transform your world. We speak words, not with very much intention nowadays. We speak words because we want to hear our own voices. We speak words because we want others to know our opinions. We speak words just because we think we're supposed to have something to say. We speak jokingly. We speak with criticism. We speak with harshness. We speak to argue.

There is so much power behind the words we speak, yet many do not consider the source from which these choices of words derive. Where does the development of the thoughts that become phrases and sentences that we speak, come from? Well, it comes from the words that we ourselves hear, read and take in. What would happen if people were so much more intentional about the words they read? The words they listen to?

About 17 years ago, I started intentionally collecting quotes. Quotes of men and women I knew nothing about. I had no clue of their existence or their expertise. I just developed an interest in recording quotes from books, magazine articles, or websites that provided encouragement. I can recall that the first time I really tried capturing words that had an impact on me was in church when I was much younger. Whenever I would come across scriptures that were important to remember, I would jot them down on my BlackBerry at the time and I just created a long extensive list of scriptures. Initially, I thought the encouragement I received from spiritual texts was satisfying, yet as I began reading a variety of books aside from my Bible, I became more open to my mind and spirit being edified by a variety of sources. I kind of became obsessed, if being obsessed with empowering quotes could be a thing. I took words from my favorite magazines and websites. I started noticing quotes from people of impact who were both alive and ancestors. The list that began as a list of scriptures also became a list of empowering and inspirational quotes.

I really focused on finding words that not only made me feel good but ones that I knew would provide some type of encouragement in the future when I needed it most. I became one of those people who would not only write down or type up quotes, but I've started to memorize them.

I would type up quotes, print them out, frame them, and put them on my walls. Sometimes I would even just cut the words and tape them around my room. Whenever I had an office at work, I would constantly place posts everywhere. It became very anchoring at times, to just sit or lie in silence and look around my room and see empowering words. After going thru many phones, I decided to just create documents with my quotes, and I can say the list has grown exponentially. I have been collecting quotes for nearly 20 years, and now, I even organize the quotes into categories. After realizing how much centeredness and peace my quotes brought me, along with the quantity I collected over the years, I decided to share some of them. I would share my favorite quotes and affirmations. Here you are.

LIFE WISDOM

❝

Life is like an ever-shifting kaleidoscope: a slight change and all patterns alter.

- SHARON SALZBERG

Our perspective shapes our life experiences. Our perspective impacts our view of ourselves, others, opportunities, and freedoms. Consider that people around you have different perspectives, thus live different lives. What would it mean if you allowed your perspective to change?

❝

Fear less, hope more, eat less, chew more, whine less, breathe more, talk less, say more, hate less, love more, and good things will be yours.

- SWEDISH PROVERB

It's possible to do less of some things and more of others. Do less of that which takes away from the beauty of life, and more that adds to experiencing life in an intentional, magical, and connected way.

❝

Life is a hard battle anyway. If we laugh and sing a little as we fight the good fight of freedom, it makes it all go easier. I will not allow my life's light to be determined by the darkness around me.

- SOJOURNER TRUTH

Our perspective shapes our life experiences. Our perspective impacts our view of ourselves, others, opportunities, and freedoms. Consider that people around you have different perspectives, thus live different lives. What would it mean if you allowed your perspective to change?

Darkness is found in the perils of human behavior: corruption, war, oppression, poverty, and social injustices. The reality of these occurrences can create a mental prison, but embracing small acts of laughter, play, and pleasure can create a sense of freedom.

The road less traveled is to understand that life is made up of opposition and learning how to live with and thru it. There are so many approaches to dealing with the troubled times that life offers. Many individuals fall into the depth of the darkness, but how glorious it would be to take light with you on the journey.

Believe that life is worth living and your belief will help create the fact.

- WILLIAM JAMES

We are not all dealt the same hand, and many times, a sense of hopelessness and helplessness consumes individuals as the monotony of life casts a shadow over their life.

Do not dwell in the past; do not dream of
the future, concentrate the mind on the present.

- BUDDHA

The past can serve a purpose. Looking into the future can be helpful. However, dwelling between either is not helpful. Being present allows us to be connected to what's happening around us. Being present allows us to be mindful of what we do, how we do it, and what is going on in our lives.

It is better to fall short of a high mark than to reach a low one

- HC Payne

Effort matters, and the more effort you make towards a goal, the more growth you experience as a person. Who you become in efforts to reach goals, is just as important as the goal itself. Reach as high as possible, and the reach will get you farther than setting a goal you know you could have attained.

Every man dies. Not every man really lives.

-Walt Whitman

Life can be looked at as more than an opportunity to just show up, handle responsibilities, and die. It can be looked at as an opportunity to have a dynamic variety of experiences. There are people who go thru life not taking risks, not exploring themselves, not exploring the world around them, and not living from a place of intention or purpose. There are many people that die feeling unfulfilled.

The future is no more uncertain than the present.

-WALT WHITMAN

We often experience anxiety or worry, however, the truth is, we do not really know the future. Every moment that passes becomes the past. Likewise, every moment in the future that comes to our consciousness then becomes the present. So, count it with a sense of comfort; at the present moment, you didn't know what would occur.

Your test becomes your testimony.

- JOEL OSTEEN

It helps to find meaning in the purpose of life. In life, an outlook on hard times allows us to connect to our own resiliency. There is a difference between seeing life as a happening to us versus for us.

❝

Everything that has a beginning has an ending. Make your peace with that and all will be well.

- BUDDHA

It's important to remember that nothing is permanent, and everything passes. As the Buddhist way would suggest, when we are too attached to what exists, there is an experience of suffering. However, the ability to appreciate what's present while allowing it the space to be released from your life is very important.

❝

Do not lose hope. Please believe that there are a thousand beautiful things waiting for you. Sunshine comes to all who feel rain.

- R.M. DRAKE

It's important to hold on to encouragement that allows you to hope for something on the other side of difficulty. Connecting to metaphors found in nature is a wonderful teacher for us. Understanding that life, as nature, has seasons, can provide a sense of hope when one is feeling stuck and hopeless.

"

What you get by achieving your goals is not as important

as what you become by achieving your goals.

- HENRY DAVID THOREAU

Getting consumed with the thought of achieving a goal and obtaining desires distracts us from being present to the opportunity of growth required in order to obtain the very goals we set. Every step you take, and every path taken, help to shape who you are as a person.

"

It's your road and yours alone. Others may walk it with you,

but no one can walk it for you.

- RUMI

Human connection is important. Support and encouragement are necessary. However, no matter who is surrounding you, your life will in many ways, be a reflection of your choices. No one can live life for you. It doesn't matter the insight, enlightenment or knowledge you've received from others, it is your decisions that shape your life outcomes.

“

**Life isn't about waiting for the storm to pass,
it's about learning to dance in the rain.**

- UNKNOWN

People often use the phrase "when." I do "xyz when", "ill feel better, when…" Let's not wait for time, and allow ourselves to find gratitude as much as possible in each moment, even during the times and seasons when it seems that no light exists.

“

From a small seed, a mighty trunk may grow

- AESCHYLUS

Every life has its beginning. There is a process that must be respected. There is time and maturation which must be respected. Even the tallest trees began as a seedling. Learn to be open to progression. Learn to be patient.

All life is an experiment. The more experiments you make, the better

- RALPH WALDO EMERSON

It feels more comfortable to not take risks; however, no matter how much information you have, life is about risks. It is about exploring and testing what you know to be true. The more you approach it like a scientist exploring a new theory, the more insight you develop.

A wise man will make more opportunities than he finds

- FRANCIS BACON

Opportunity isn't always presented in the way we want it to be; therefore, we must know that opportunity can also be the space and freedom to create.

66

The only real failure in life is not to be true to the best one knows.

What is life if you journeyed through it not being connected to yourself, embracing who you are, or even living authentically? Living life to fulfill others' expectations and ideals, rather than living in a way that would allow you to embrace who you really are is often an unfulfilled life.

66

Life shrinks or expands in proportion to one's courage

The more chances and risks you take, the more opportunities you go for, the more vulnerable you are, and the more experiences you have. When you choose safe, you live safe, which is fine; however, if you want to experience possibility beyond what you can conceive, find ways to consistently challenge yourself, step outside the line, and be bold to do what doesn't seem comfortable.

A journey of a thousand miles must begin with a single step.

- LAO TZU

Every step matters. When you have a destination in mind, you can get so overwhelmed by what it takes to get there. You may doubt your skillset, knowledge, strength, or tenacity, but all that matters is that you take the first step, and work on one step at a time.

Your work is to discover your work and then with all your heart to give yourself to it.

- BUDDHA

In pursuit of "success", people can fall into or choose a vocation or career based on circumstance or stability, but true work comes when you can connect what you do to your spirit. Connect to the notion of your soul's work, which is the higher calling or gift someone can connect to that supports, encourages, heals, or helps other people. When you discover what your soul work is, it's important to devote as much time and energy as possible to it, because remember, what you do, affects others.

"

Always be yourself, express yourself, have faith in yourself, do not go out and look for a successful personality and duplicate it.

- BRUCE LEE

You as an individual are unique. There is no need to diminish who you are in order to be like someone else. No one else is duplicatable, just as you are not duplicatable.

"

If you can't live longer, live deeper.

- ITALIAN PROVERB

There is no control over the length of life you're able to live. Therefore, use the time you have wisely to live your best life, whatever that means to you. Live with purpose, live with intention, live with an authentic connection to yourself and others.

❝❝

A bird does not sing because it has an answer.

It sings because it has a song..

- CHINESE PROVERB

Release and share with the world what is inside of you. What is inside of you has been planted for you to nurture and share.

❝❝

Those who wish to sing always find a song.

- SWEDISH PROVERB

If one follows their gifts and desires, they will make a way to express themselves or make their desires come true. When something is really inside of you, it is difficult to ignore it. Allow your ideas and gifts to come to life.

＂

It's not enough to learn how to ride, you must also learn how to fall.

- MEXICAN PROVERB

Learn to accept defeat. Acceptance is the core of self-love Acceptance is learning to embrace who you are when you've won, as well as learning to embrace who you are when you feel like you've failed.

＂

Your time is limited, so don't waste it living someone else's life.

- STEVE JOBS

Honoring who you are, means being able to honor the life you have, honoring what you like and honoring what you want to change. Your life is your own and feeling the need to live someone else's life almost diminishes and demeans the presence of your existence.

“

Life is not a problem to be solved, but a reality to be experienced.

- SOREN KIERKEGAARD

If you have any ounce of perfectionism, idealism or romanticism in you, it's possible to always look at life from a solutions-focused perspective. Often assessing how to make it better, and changing what's going on to fit your ideals; however, sometimes, life is just supposed to be lived and faced.

“

We make a living by what we get. We make a life by what we give.

-WINSTON CHURCHILL

There is a different life experience when we live from a place of philanthropy, service or impact, rather than focusing on what one can obtain. Each of us has the capacity to effect another person, and with intentionality, can benefit our community if we keep that in mind. It means very little to acquire everything one wants, and not share it with anyone. We want much, but actually need very little as individuals.

No one escapes life without some experience of feeling miserable, sad, hurt, or disappointed. We all have this truth in common; however, everyone's wounds are not visible. Remember that everyone has a battle they're fighting or has had a battle they have fought.

When we don't deem ourselves worthy enough of being authentic, we will unconsciously wear the masks that make us resemble the identity of others. Connect to who you are, so that you don't feel the need to be other people.

"

Not everything that is faced can be changed,
but nothing can be changed until it is faced.
- James Baldwin

Once events occur in our lives, they are in the past, and the past cannot be changed. People spend so much time regretting past choices, but it's a waste. It is like crying over spilled milk. What is advantageous is looking at choices, and deconstructing the motivation for them. If we face the truth around previous choices, we can move forward with more insight and intention.

WELLNESS AND HEALING

Renewal is what happens when you realize that some of this stuff you've been carrying around doesn't matter.

- ROB BELL

We are most impacted by the deadweight that judgement and shame bring. When we can learn to let go and accept that what is, is, then we experience a unique type of freedom that allows us to constantly release stress and feel renewed.

The greatest wealth is health.

- VIRGIL

Nothing can be more valuable than one's health. Individuals pursue wealth and possessions, yet tend to neglect their physical, mental and spiritual health in their pursuits. Often, people attain what they want, however, their health suffers as a result.

❝

Go inward and inquire, and you will see that all your miseries exist because you support them. Without your support, nothing can exist. Because you give it energy, it exists; if you don't give it energy, it cannot exist.

- OSHO

Our thoughts are core to the foundation of our emotional experience. Whatever we lend our attention to, expands, be it positive, negative, helpful or maladaptive. If you are looking to do any type of healing worth, working on your thoughts is a very important step.

❝

When we heal ourselves, we heal the next generation that follows. Pain is passed through the family line until someone is ready to feel it, heal it and let it go.

- ADYASHANTI

We are constantly affecting and shaping those around us. We have the power to positively or negatively impact someone, whether intentionally or unintentionally. When one is intentional about healing, they are stepping into a space of awareness and accountability that can end behavioral cycles, and thought patterns that may have kept a family emotionally, physically, mentally or spiritually imprisoned and wounded. The change in your family can begin with you.

You are as important to your health as it is to you

- TERRI GUILLEMETS

Health is not just about a physical state. Health is all-encompassing of yourself; self-esteem, self-perception, and your identity. Your health encompasses the inner workings of your psychological, physical, and spiritual state.

Peace comes from within. Do not seek it without

- BUDDHA

On a journey of healing, one may seek peace in spiritual practices, self-care regimes, or environments. However, peace is a state that comes from within, no matter what is going on outside of you.

Life is not merely being alive, but being well.
- MARCUS VALERIUS MARTIAL

Anyone could be alive and experience a poor quality of life, utter regret or sadness about being alive; their physical health and mental health could be in such disarray, that they could be barely surviving. If you have breath in your body, be intentional about how you live your life. Living life is about your choices, your relationship with yourself and others, your physical state, and your sense of self.

❝

Be more meditative, become more conscious of your being. Let your inner world become more silent, and love will be flowing through you.
- OSHO

Stillness is something very difficult for many people to practice because of all the distraction that exists. Becoming focused on one's internal state, as well as the occurrences of the present, allows you to be really connected to the presence of your full self. The more stillness you incorporate, the more silence that can exist in your mind, and a connection to what feels like love, can occur.

Health is a relationship between you and your body

- TERRI GUILLEMETS

Because health really encompasses multiple dimensions like the mental, physical, emotional, spiritual, and financial, ultimately, health is an overall snapshot of our environment, decisions, and lifestyle.

Just as a candle cannot burn without fire, men

cannot live without a spiritual life.

- BUDDHA

Something has to motivate you, something has to ignite the fire within you, something helps you connect to your purpose, something keeps you anchored to your higher consciousness, and that is a sense of spirituality. Spirituality is an understanding of higher functioning and an interconnectedness of being.

❝

The cure for the pain is in the pain.

- RUMI

We often want to escape pain, but fail to realize that pain serves a purpose, many lessons, and an opportunity for transformation. Pain is never an enjoyable experience; however, it presents wisdom that we wouldn't gather otherwise.

❝

I've found that the changes I feared would ruin me have always become

doorways, and on the other side, I have found a

more courageous and graceful self.

- ELIZABETH LESSER

We are often afraid of the unknown, and sometimes our fear is that we will be changed for the worst. However, change is necessary, and if we learn to embrace the beauty of change, we can see ourselves transform and become individuals we didn't know were possible.

Everything matters. Everything that has happened to you has shaped you. Therefore, move forward from the end of a period in your life, from the completion of a relationship, from the lessons you have learned, with gratitude. Choose to not walk in bitterness, resentment or regret. Take with you into the future positive energy and gratitude. Learn to be grateful for all past experiences, especially the hurtful ones.

It takes a certain type of strength and courage to step up and open ourselves up to change. It takes courage to practice vulnerability and admit that you can be better or different in some kind of way.

“

The wound is the place where light enters you.
- RUMI

Our greatest strengths come from our biggest and deepest wounds.

“

Healing takes courage, and we all have courage,
even if we have to dig a little to find it
- TORI AMOS

Healing is achieved through intentionally releasing and facing the wounds. We all have the capacity for healing, especially since we all have the ability to be courageous.

“

Eventually, you will come to understand that
love heals everything, and love is all there is.
- Gary Zukov

Life wisdom said that everything comes back to love or fear. If any part of you requires healing or restoration, it is the act of love from within or from another that can shift whatever is going on.

“

The concept of total wellness recognizes that our every thought, word, and
behavior affect our greater health and well-being. And we, in turn, are affected
not only emotionally but also physically and spiritually.
- Greg Anderson

Wellness operates on the notion of holistic interaction. Knowing that every ounce of our being is connected can lead one into understanding how much each dimension of our being, affects another. You cannot properly heal one part of your being, as another part is suffering.

**The ability to be in the present moment is a major
component of mental wellness.**
- ABRAHAM MASLOW

Being aware of and connected to the present is important to one's sense of overall wellness. Being able to be present is an indication that anxiety and worry are low, that one has control and connection to the mind, and that one can connect to and understand the importance of groundedness. Pre-occupation with both the present and the past

Those who are free of resentful thoughts surely find peace.
- BUDDHA

Resentment, bitterness, anger, and frustration, are lower-frequency emotions that typically rob of internal peace. However, emotions are meant to be felt. Thoughts, on the other hand, can disrupt our welfare.

Existence already accepts you-that's why you are here. Otherwise, you would

not be. This is my basic teaching to you. Existence already accepts you. You do

not have to earn it, you are already worthy. Relax,

enjoy the way nature has made you.

- OSHO

Many spend their lives trying to prove to themselves and others that they are enough. There is a concept of working towards being deserving of love, relationships, possessions, and opportunities. However, if one reaches enlightenment, there is a realization that your worthiness is inherent to your being.

To keep the body in good health is a duty, otherwise, we shall

not be able to keep our mind strong and clear.

- BUDDHA

The status of our mental health is very well connected to our physical health. We must not neglect our physical health because by acquiring illnesses and complications, we will also compromise our peace of mind.

66

Worry and rumination do not only interrupt the quality of our lives but also add unnecessary stress. Stress is the major culprit for any chronic illnesses and immunity conditions that compromise our physical strength. Worry and rumination also feed into anxiety, a mental illness condition. Being present just allows one to be connected to what is.

66

Wellness is a concept that must be considered holistically. Therefore, you cannot truly evaluate someone's health based on one aspect of their health.

"

So many people spend their health gaining wealth, and then have to spend
their wealth to regain their health..
- A.J. Reb Materi

Due to asset, material and wealth accumulation being a priority
for many, they often sacrifice their health in lieu of their
search. When one focuses more on their goals and career by
sacrificing essentials like sleep, and balanced nutrition, there
is a price to pay for not monitoring health.

"

Health is a state of complete physical, mental and social well-being, and not
merely the absence of disease or infirmity.
- World Health Organization

Understanding that the status of our overall health is composed
of many aspects of our lives, it is important to consider what
health means holistically, which includes our emotional and
mental state. It includes our ability to interact with others, and
how we are affected by others.

❝

Even though anger is a primary emotion, and is meant to be experienced, how often one experiences it, is indicative of their emotional health. It is important to pay attention to how often this emotion lingers, and in what capacity. Be mindful of the circumstances and thoughts that you're anger is tied to. It can be detrimental to one's mental state, therefore focusing on releasing the thoughts connected to it, is essential.

❝

It seems easier to have a sense of self when you are comfortable; however, when you are uncomfortable during a moment, an environment, or a season in your life, that is the time when your true self reveals itself. When what keeps you comfortable leaves, that is when you begin to ask yourself questions. In asking yourself questions, you can peel back the layers of who you thought you were, and who exists outside of that.

Out of suffering have emerged the strongest souls; the most massive characters are seared with scars.

- **KHALIL GIBRAN**

It seems that difficulties, tribulations, and pain stretches the human mind and expands the spirit. As much as suffering can leave a scar, it increases the tolerance of one who survives it. It builds up the muscle and endurance of the one who was able to go thru the time. It is not possible to have a sense of mental and emotional strength, without bearing scars.

LOVE

When we are loving, we openly and honestly express care, affection, responsibility, respect, commitment, and trust.

- BELL HOOKS

The feeling of love is very much connected with the notion of safety. When we feel safe, we feel open to express ourselves. Consider that when it comes to any relationship in which you feel someone is not safe for you to be yourself with, or be open, how much love is in it?

There is always something to do. There are hungry people to feed, naked people to clothe, and sick people to comfort and make well. And while I don't expect you to save the world, I do think it's not asking too much for you to love those with whom you sleep, share the happiness of those whom you call friends, engage those among you who are visionary and remove from your life those who offer you depression, despair and disrespect.

- KHALIL GIBRAN

Love is an abundant resource that we share with scarcity. It would make an impact in the world, if everyone felt loved, and received the love they needed to thrive. Consider what steps you need to take, to give more love, and remove toxicity from your life. When we don't feel love, we cause pain to others, thus continuing a cycle of a deficit of love.

Connecting to the possibility of love, the comfort that comes with love, the peace that comes with love, or the joy that comes with love, expands our experience in this world. Once you receive something so rich, it expands the type of experience you want to have in all dimensions of your life. Those who seem attached to lower-frequency emotional experiences do not know what it is like to not live out of fear, but those who connect to love, do. Love does not begin and end the way we seem to think it does.

❝

Love is a battle; love is a war; love is a growing up
- JAMES BALDWIN

There tends to be a very romantic, and stress-free association that comes with love; however, true love brings about uncomfortable transformation, it uncovers pain, releases strife, and takes a maturity that many don't acquire. Love is experienced with imperfect humans that bring their imperfections, wounds and fears to the relationships.

❝

Your task is not to seek for love, but merely to seek and find all the barriers within yourself that you have built against it.
- ANONYMOUS

All the things you need, are in you. Take heed of the life that leads you on a journey of looking for love outside of yourself. Take heed if you're looking for someone to fill voids within you that require introspection and healing on your own behalf.

"

To love well is the task in all meaningful relationships,

not just romantic bonds..

- BELL HOOKS

Love is a fundamental experience when relationshipping with anyone. As love embodies patience, understanding, empathy, support, openness and trust, meaningful relationships require these dynamics and more.

"

Where there is love, there is no darkness.

- BURUNDI PROVERB

Love represents light. In love, there is hope, peace, joy, gratitude, and compassion. These are virtues that heal. These are virtues that illuminate our human experience, which is why, if there is love, there is no darkness.

❝

Darkness cannot drive out darkness; only light can do that.

Hate cannot drive out hate; only love can do that

- MARTIN LUTHER KING JR.

Opposition is necessary. Dark does not exist without light and vice versa. An element of the same kind, cannot provide any movement or dissipation and needs an opposing element for a reaction.

❝

Never go in search for love, go in search of life,

and life will find you the love you seek.

- ATTICUS

When one is living life from a place of exploration, curiosity and fulfillment, all that could be granted to you, will find its way to you. Live your journey, and all that is meant to enhance your life will be added to you. You do not have to go in search of it.

**Being deeply loved by someone gives you strength
while loving someone deeply gives you courage.**
- LAO TZU

Finding the space in our hearts to be vulnerable and open to love requires a hint of courage and bravery. Vulnerability is often seen as a weakness, but it shows true strength and connection to one's self.

**I have learned not to worry about love;
But to honor its coming with all my heart.**
- ALICE WALKER

To return to love, to get the love we always wanted but never had, to have the love we want but are not prepared to give, we seek romantic relationships. We believe these relationships, more than any other, will rescue and redeem us. True love does have the power to redeem but only if we are ready for redemption. Love saves us only if we want to be saved.

- BELL HOOKS

PATIENCE

There is pleasure in the pathless woods

- LORD BYRON

If one practices patience and is open to learning, not having a clear sense of direction can be a journey of discovery and pleasant surprises.

From a small seed, a mighty trunk may grow

- AESCHYLUS

We never really know what is to come out of an idea, an opportunity, etc. A seed represents something that has infinite possibilities, but it takes time to witness the unfolding of said possibilities.

"

Truth is more valuable if it takes you a few years to find it.

In growth and wisdom, there is something very valuable about the understanding that time gives us that cannot be replaced by just hearing or reading in one moment in time. It seems that if you are on a journey, and are present on the journey, it is time that helps to reveal all.

"

Patience is bitter, but its fruit is sweet.

Engaging in any experience that would require patience or bring about a challenge of temperance is an experience that could seem difficult and challenging, however, is one that has a reward set in growth, maturity, and strength.

It is easier to find men who will volunteer to die.

Than to find those who are willing to endure pain with patience.

- JULIUS CAESAR

Death is an endpoint. Most people want the easiest and shortest way out of struggle. It is difficult to power through the test of time to reach a victory. The lack of patience is often why people give up on their goals and aspirations. It takes a different type of strength to endure challenges for an extended period.

Be strong enough to let go and wise enough to wait for what you deserve.

- ANONYMOUS

Learning to discern what is worth releasing, and what is worth sticking out for the desired result can be complicated. It is important to constantly search within yourself where your motivation to let go or hold on is coming from. Everything won't come to you easily or swiftly, however, everything nor everyone is not meant to stay with you either.

So many of the tests we face are centered around basic virtues like patience. Understanding the importance of time and "trusting the process" is really essential to allowing life to unfold. Those who lack patience often have a strenuous relationship with control. Over-relying on one's ability to control life can often result in a sense of disharmony.

There are so many distractions that can pull us away from a life that we desire or are willed to experience. Impatience is one of the greatest distractions because we become enamored by the destination and intolerant of the journey. People all around you can give up on something because of age, time, life circumstances, transitions, etc., but it can be your patience and understanding of the commitment to something, that keeps you going. There is no rush; no matter how many people tell you the time is now.

"

Patience attracts happiness; it brings near that which is far.

- SWAHILI PROVERB

There is something special about someone who has the capability of being patient. They often may have less doubt, worry or anxiety. They have with them an internal state of faith and belief that waiting and accepting the now for what it is, is ok. They don't feel like they are missing out and create a pathway to create more joy to be in the present.

"

All great achievements require time.

- MAYA ANGELOU

Technology has fooled the average human into believing that most of what we want can be instantly and readily available to us. Even though technology creates experiences of instant satisfaction, this is not the reality. To even get to the point of the technological advancements we have, it has taken a collection of centuries for innovators to build off the knowledge of one another. Consider that the people you admire most spent their whole lives becoming the person you admire.

There is something good in all seeming failures.
You are not to see that now. Time will reveal it. Be patient.
- SIVANANDA SARASWATI

Being that hindsight is 20/20, there is often insight and understanding that one does not receive until after a life experience or circumstance has passed. It sometimes takes time for the pieces of our life's puzzle to come together.

I think you have to try and fail because
failure gets you closer to what you're good at.
- LOUIS C.K.

Every attempt towards a goal gets you closer to the goal. Often times, failure or shortcomings can be seen as barriers. Who you become, and what you learn on the way to the goal matter just as much as meeting the goal.

"

Practicing patience doesn't feel pleasurable but the outcome is rewarding.

- FRENCH PROVERB

Practicing patience doesn't feel pleasurable but the outcome is rewarding.

FAITH

> **“**
>
> Optimism is the faith that leads to achievement.
> Nothing can be done without hope and confidence.
>
> — HELEN KELLER

One has to believe in the possibility of achievement to work towards achievement. Hope and belief drive the human spirit, therefore without them, it would be difficult to attain much.

> **“**
>
> Keep your dreams alive. Understand to achieve anything requires faith and belief in yourself, vision, hard work, determination, and dedication. Remember all things are possible for those who believe.
>
> — GAIL DEVERS

In my deepest, darkest moments, what really got me through was a prayer. Sometimes my prayer was 'Help me.' Sometimes a prayer was 'Thank you.' What I've discovered is that intimate connection and communication with my creator will always get me through because I know my support, my help, is just a prayer away

- IYANLA VANZANT

Having a connection to a spirituality identity can provide a greater context to life in ways that we cannot comprehend. It becomes psychologically beneficial to hold on to something when in despair. This experience of hope is what encourages mental strength, tenacity and grit.

The foundation stones for a balanced success are honesty, character, integrity, faith, love and loyalty.

- ZIG ZIGLAR

Success is a reflection of inner work. Balanced success is the success that is not rooted in greed or ego.

❝

Begin to weave and God will give the thread
- GERMAN PROVERB

Doing work, and believing in power or synchronicity of events beyond yourself can really provide encouragement and a reminder that you are not in control of everything. However, just sitting back will not put what you need into motion.

❝

In three words, I can sum up everything I've learned about life: it goes on.
- ROBERT FROST

We become so attached to the remnants of the past. We create suffering within ourselves when we sulk over failures and loss. We get caught up in circumstances that create feelings of shame, embarrassment or guilt. However, life continues. We get ourselves stuck in a moment of time when in truth, everything continues to move forward. For your own sense of mental health, acknowledge your emotions, feel them, but don't sit in them, or experiences of life. Move on, learn lessons, shift what's necessary, take action, or let go.

"

Believe in the transformation of your experiences. Nature tends to provide us with some of the greatest lessons, and seeing the beauty or at minimum, the purpose and value of change is important. Believing that there is light after or even in the midst of darkness, is a supreme gesture of faith.

"

Faith is an active word that allows us to not only be connected to possibilities but also guides us into interacting in a world in which we have been told to only trust our senses. There is much that we move through our days in faith around. We have faith that we will get to work, or our destination safely. We have faith that everyone connected to us is living. We have faith in so much that we can't see, yet the belief or assumption keeps life moving.

Without faith, nothing is possible. With it, nothing is impossible.
- MARY MCLEOD BETHUNE

There has to be an underlying belief in whatever you're doing. Whatever you set forth in your mind brings about or takes away possibility. It would serve you to have faith in your desires.

It's lack of faith that makes people afraid of meeting challenges,
and I believed in myself.
- MUHAMMAD ALI

Faith comes in handy when you are facing something that brings about fear. When fear arises, we convince ourselves to walk away from opportunities. We convince ourselves to make decisions that are ruled by comfort. However, faith, in the midst of fear allows us to shock ourselves. It puts us in a position to make things we previously thought of as unimaginable, as beyond possible.

Our mind can be our best friend or our worst enemy. Know when your mind is your enemy, and being entangled in your thoughts can threaten your well-being.

As impatient as we may grow sometimes to "fix" ourselves as fast as possible, it's important to know that your healing has its own appointed time. Learn to not only be patient with your healing but also gentle and compassionate.

“

Turn your demons into art, your shadow into a friend, your fear into fuel, your failures into teachers, your weaknesses into reasons to keep fighting. Don't waste your pain. Recycle your heart.

Everything that we receive in life can be used with purpose. Every perceived experience of darkness or hurt can be repurposed into a tool of light. Our perspective and reaction to life are what allow us to re-define our experiences in a way that empowers us.

“

Sometimes our own needs and desires must be expressed, even at the expense of shattering the image others have created of us.
- SEAN WOLFE

The easiest way to silence ourselves is to forget we have a voice. Allowing the fear of consequence or judgement to get in the way of you asserting your needs can become dangerous.

"

You don't have to be positive all the time. It's perfectly okay to feel sad, angry, annoyed, frustrated, scared and anxious. Having feelings doesn't make you a negative person. It makes you human.

- LORI DESCHENE

Learning to practice radical acceptance of what is, allows us to accept our true selves.

GOALS, DREAMS AND DETERMINATION

“

Fall seven times, stand up eight.

- Japanese proverb

No matter how many times you feel like you fail, keep getting back up, and doing your best. If you feel down, do what needs to be done to get yourself on your feet. It doesn't mean it has to be alone, but do what needs to be done.

“

Turn your face toward the sun and the shadows fall behind you.

- Maori proverb

When you look forward, the very darkness that may be overshadowing your life will at some point be behind you. Allow optimism to push you thru the times that seem most difficult because eventually, those times will be a part of your past.

❝

Some men go through a forest and see no firewood.

- ENGLISH PROVERB

Perception is key, and it's important to understand that everyone doesn't see the same opportunities that life has to offer.

❝

I can accept failure, everyone fails at something.
But I cannot accept not trying..

- MICHAEL JORDON

It is better to try at something and fail rather than to not try at all because at least, with failure, there is an opportunity to learn. Avoidance brings no opportunities for growth or insight.

“

Whenever you want to achieve something, keep your eyes open, concentrate and make sure you know exactly what it is you want. No one can hit their target with their eyes closed.

- PAULO COELHO

It takes focus and awareness to move towards a goal. There is a fine balance between visualization, intention, openness to possibility, and concentrated efforts. It's important to know that you have power and impact while not being too involved in controlling your life circumstances.

“

It's not the load that breaks you down, it's the way you carry it.

- LENA HORNE

Perception and resources heavily impact how we are able to maneuver the world with the challenges that we have. Two people can have the same "load" in terms of challenges, but with differing perspectives and use of resources, they could handle the load differently. Learn to be a realistic optimist. Try to look at the lesson or advantage of your challenges. Also, learn to receive support and assistance, or leverage the strength of others to manage the load you do have.

Winning is great, sure, but if you are really going to do something in life, the secret is learning how to lose. Nobody goes undefeated all the time. If you can pick up after a crushing defeat, and go on to win again, you are going to be a champion someday.

- WILMA RUDOLPH

A true test of grit is what happens when something doesn't go your way. Some people see losing as defeat, but others can view it as an opportunity for growth. You will not always receive what you want. You will not always be in the green. You won't always be number one. Therefore learn how to accept all positions in life. Take it with grace, and do what you need to do, to perform at your greatest potential.

You may encounter many defeats, but you must not be defeated. In fact, it may be necessary to encounter the defeats, so you can know who you are, what you can rise from, how you can still come out of it

- MAYA ANGELOU

Taking defeat teaches us about ourselves. We come to terms with how we accept life. We see how much we can face, and what lengths we go to, to build ourselves up. You can gage how strong your mind is when defeat occurs.

66

The triumph can't be had without the struggle.

- WILMA RUDOLPH

To win, triumph, or overcome anything, it will always take work and what feels like some type of struggle. To win, one must stretch themselves beyond their current capacity. There will be tests of willpower and willingness. There will be a need for discipline, to push.

66

You will be wounded many times in your life. You'll make mistakes. Some people will call them failures, but I have learned that failure is really God's way of saying, "Excuse me, you're moving in the wrong direction." It's just an experience, just an experience.

- OPRAH WINFREY

Be wary of taking failures, defeats, losses, and anything that seems like an unfortunate circumstance as a sign of personal deficit. All experiences provide insight. All experiences provide an opportunity for growth. You won't always have the answers, and of course, everything seems easier to understand in hindsight.

“

The ultimate measure of a man is not where he stands in moments of comfort and convenience, but where he stands at times of challenge and controversy.

- DR. MARTIN LUTHER KING JR.

When faced with conflict, disagreement, injustice, or complete discomfort, a true test of character arises. It's easy to make ideal decisions when one is comfortable; but it is the fire, the heat, or the pressure that one faces which provides true insight into who someone is, when it matters, and convenience is not an option.

“

Never give up, for that is the place and time where the tide will turn.

- DR. MARTIN LUTHER KING JR.

It always seems that every event or major season in our lives has a tipping pint. The tipping is the point at which energy shifts. It's the point of significance in which what existed will naturally find balance in the universe and present as its opposite. Therefore, the notion of a climax is often written in plays and films because it is a representation of what happens in life.

❝

Reach high for stars lie hidden in your soul.

Dream deep, for every dream precedes the goal.

- PAMELA VAULL STARR

It is important to be connected to something within or beyond that can drive you. Something that drives impact, passion, or change in this world.

❝

Vision is the art of seeing what is invisible to others.

- JONATHAN SWIFT

Vision takes connection to a higher sense of self. Vision takes on a supernatural quality for it is based on that which does not exist and that which often seems unattainable to others. This is why vision is often given to leaders or a special appointed person. Visions are uniquely given and can only be cast from one being at a time.

Every great dream begins with a dreamer. Always remember, you have within you the strength, the patience, and the passion to reach for the stars to change the world.

- HARRIET TUBMAN

Mostly, everything you see around you was the result of a vision: your furniture, your dwellings, your appliances, your mode of transportation, and this book. There's power within and around you to bring forth dreams and visions, but it takes patience and a connection to the idea to make it come to pass.

Dreams seldom materialize on their own.

- DIAN FOSSEY

Action is always necessary to transform your dreams into fruition. Action consists of steps you make, as well as the steps others make to bring forth any vision or idea. It's always a process.

❝

If you can imagine it, you can create it. If you can dream it, you can become it

- WILLIAM ARTHUR WARD

The mind is powerful, and it tends to create anything that can come to pass. If you are to believe in infinite intelligence, then you could see how infinite intelligence surrounds and influences us.

❝

Always go with your passions. Never ask yourself if it's realistic or not.

- DEEPAK CHOPRA

Your passions can take you places, open up doors, and impact that world in a way that realism may not. Passions may not always play out how we want them to, however, fire exists within you for reason. Follow that and share it with the world.

You are not here merely to make a living. You are here in order to enable the world to live more amply, with greater vision, with a finer spirit of hope and achievement. You are here to enrich the world, and you impoverish yourself if you forget the errand

- WOODROW WILSON

There is much to do with one's life beyond the repetition and routine that comes with falling into the mundane. If one focuses only on working and surviving, there is no space for giving, for love, for exploration, for creativity or for expression. It is our movement beyond routine that allows us to create a life worth living.

Your vision will become clear only when you can look into your own heart. Who looks outside, dreams; who looks inside, awakes.

- CARL JUNG

There's a unique infinite intelligence that dwells within us all, and the potential to harness the power within you and give to the world can only be tapped into when you are connected with yourself. It's one thing to make goals and envision your world based on what you see, yet it is something else to create based on what has been revealed in you.

It may be that those who do most, dream most

- STEPHEN LEACOCK

When you repeatedly have visions for your life, it can propel you to put effort into taking chances and going after opportunities. Visions and dreams can keep us motivated to take action in our life.

Some people see things as they are and ask why?

Others dream things that never were and ask why not?

- GEORGE BERNARD SHAW

Consider the many inventions and innovations that have marked our human experience. It means a lot to step outside of the limits and boxes that seem to already exist and question what could be different. The difference between what exists today versus what didn't exist in the past is taking action based on the question, why?

It is never too late to be what you might have been

We often put time constraints on our dreams, and sometimes our goals. After we pass the point at which we imagined certain dreams or goals coming to pass, we release them and walk away. We may continue living life, thinking about what if, and grieving the dream that we once had. Understand that if you have time and energy to pursue what it is you once held on to, you can be what you thought, it was too late to be.

The depth of your struggle determines the height of your success

Sometimes it feels like the challenges we face in life are in vain, however, if you keep staying focused on the journey ahead, you will find an inverse relationship between what you went thru and how much prosperity, impact or achievement you experience.

**Success is the ability to go from failure
to failure without losing your enthusiasm
- WINSTON CHURCHILL**

It's easier to basque in the initial excitement about a project or goal than to maintain that fervency even after you fall a couple of times. Getting thru times of challenge and what one feels like failure is essential to strengthening yourself and understanding how life works.

**Nothing will work unless you do.
- MAYA ANGELOU**

What you want doesn't just happen; it's your actions, choices and work that put things in motion.

“

In great attempts, it is even glorious to fail.

- VINCENT T. LOMBARDI

The notion of failure, to a great extent, is an indicator of effort and striving towards something. Even with large goals and dreams, it means more to try and get somewhere than to never pursued the object of your desire.

“

First say to yourself what would you be, and then do what you need to do

- EPICTETUS

Sometimes requirements and thinking of an expected journey to a goal can be overwhelming and disparaging, therefore, take the time to first think about what you want to do and why. In moving forward, you can be tunnel visioned by staying focused on what you want to become.

RELATIONSHIPS - THE TEAM, THE GROUP, FRIENDS

❝

Finding good players is easy. Getting them to play as a team is another story.

- CASEY STENGEL

It's easier for most people to be great in solitude rather than to learn how to work with others and be even greater. There is power and uniqueness that each of us holds, however, having the ability to connect with and be in conjunction with others takes skill and understanding.

❝

Cheese, wine, and friends must be old to be good

- CUBAN PROVERB

Some experiences are about time. It is true that you can be satisfied with something made quickly. You can even be excited about someone you meant and felt a deep connection to in a short period of time. However, nothing replaces the value of time. There is power in process. In relationships, it really takes time for someone to really know you, not from a cerebral place, but from an emotional and spiritual place.

❝

Even from a foe, a man may learn wisdom

- GREEK PROVER

Do not underestimate the value that someone could add to your life. People that we dislike or do not agree with can surprisingly teach us something. Everyone around us, no matter the relationship that exists, has the capacity to be a teacher.

❝

Just as distance tests a horse's strength, time can reveal a person's heart.

- CHINESE PROVERB

It is often the passing of time that reveals the truth about someone. Be patient as you build relationships.

❝

Do not choose the one you don't trust and trust the one you chose.

- CHINESE PROVERBS

Often times our intuition can give us a different type of insight than our minds. Don't be with or work with people you don't trust. However, if you are choosing to be in a relationship with someone, give them your respect and your trust.

❝

In this life, when you deny someone an apology, you will remember it at the time you beg forgiveness.

- TOBA BETA

Whether you believe in Karma or not, know that we are eventually on the receiving end of a circumstance that we experienced at the hands of someone else. There will be times you will make decisions that negatively impact others, so be mindful of being judgmental, critical, or cold towards others.

No person is your friend who demands your silence,

or denies your right to grow.

- ALICE WALKER

Friends support one another and allow you to be yourself authentically. Health relationships are safe. Unhealthy relationships involve dishonesty, abuse, neglect, coercion, control, and manipulation.

Surround yourself with only people who are going to lift you higher.

- OPRAH WINFREY

It can be easy to overlook how others support us. It's important to have people that affirm and praise you genuinely. We look at how they make us feel but don't always look at whether they would step out of their comfort zones to encourage, empower, push or support us. Its often not until a life tragedy that we see some people in our lives don't have the capacity to lift us.

"

When a team outgrows individual performance and learns team confidence, excellence becomes a reality..
- JOE PATERNO

The true success of a team or group is reflective of the unity and confidence they have in one another as a unit.

"

It is amazing how much people get done if they do not worry about who gets the credit.
- MAYA ANGELOU

It is amazing how much people get done if they do not worry about who gets the credit. - Swahili proverb

"

A team is more than a collection of people. It is a process of give and take.
- BARBARA GLACEL& EMILE ROBERT JR.

When we work with or are in relationships with others, we learn a significant amount of information about ourselves, as well as what it actually takes to interact with others.

"

None of us is as smart as all of us.
- KEN BLANCHARD

Collective energy and intelligence can be more powerful than the intellect of one person. Everyone has blindspots and shortcomings that could be made up for by another.

"

No man is wise enough by himself.
- PLAUTUS

Wisdom is the result of experience and collective consciousness. The wisdom we learn comes from lived experiences, as well as observations, and in fact, interaction with people's thoughts and perceptions.

“

Interdependent people combine their own efforts

with the efforts of others to achieve their greatest success.

- STEPHEN COVEY

It is known that collective action is what propels "success." Whether that is working with a team, or in collaboration with someone else, true independence does not garner success.

“

The ratio of We's to I's is the best indicator of the development of a team.

- LEWIS B. ERGEN

Teams are not productive when egos overshadow the group. The more members know that their collective action and connection are more beneficial, the more a team resembles a true team.

“

One man can be a crucial ingredient on a team,
but one man cannot make a team.
- KAREEM ABDUL-JABBAR

Each member of a team matters. Some members can possess an impactful amount of skill, talent or wisdom, but no matter what, a team needs the participation of everyone to really thrive.

“

The leaders who work most effectively, it seems to me, never say 'I.' And that's not because they have trained themselves not to say 'I.' They don't think 'I.' They think 'we'; they think 'team.' They understand their job to be to make the team function. They accept responsibility and don't sidestep it, but 'we' get the credit. This is what creates trust, what enables you to get the task done.
- PETER DRUCKER

> **"**
>
> **I've learned that people will forget what you said, people will forget what you did, but people will never forget how you made them feel**
>
> **- MAYA ANGELOU**

As humans, our emotions matter; when we are working with or in a relationship with others, our well-being is often connected to emotional experience. This is why how someone makes us feel can be the best or worst thing for us. Think about the common experience of someone's heart being broken, and them never wanting to feel that again.

> **"**
>
> **Talent wins games, but teamwork and intelligence win championships..**
>
> **- MICHAEL JORDAN**

There are small battles and then there are major battles that may define a war. To make a big impact takes more than skillset, it takes work, strategy, and communication; something that comes with effective teamwork.

“

Coming together is a beginning. Keeping together
is progress. Working together is success.

- HENRY FORD

Everyone can't endure the processes of life. We may engage or be involved in the initial steps, but once time and difficulty present themselves, momentum stops, and people walk away. If you want success in any relationship, working together is key.

Teamwork is the fuel that allows common people to attain uncommon results.

- ANONYMOUS

It is collective action and support that propels an individual to perform in a way that they would not have been able to by themselves. When you see someone great, know that it's their team plus them that got them there.

❝

Teams share the burden and divide the grief.

- DOUG SMITH

When you work with others, everyone holds the weight of every aspect of a team experience. True teams know, no one person is to blame for anything. You carry weight equally and uphold each other equally.

❝

Individual commitment to a group effort - that is what makes a team work a company work, a society work, a civilization work.

- VINCE LOMBARDI

Every person in a relationship or team must give effort. It doesn't work when there is an imbalance of output.

**Build for your team a feeling of oneness, of dependence
on one another and of strength to be derived by unity
- VINCE LOMBARDI**

It takes more than a group of people to be a team; it takes connection. It takes unity. Unity has to be the foundation. If everyone feels united, then each person will support, build up, and lean on one another.

**In teamwork, silence isn't golden, it's deadly.
- MARK SANBORN**

Effective communication is essential to all relationships. In order to effectively make progress, positively deliver outcomes, and fluidly work with others, communication must occur. Lack of communication breeds confusion, doubt, and ambiguity.

"

The greatest danger a team faces isn't that it won't become successful,
but that it will, and then cease to improve.
- MARK SANBORN

Having something to work towards is important to human development and achievement. Some individuals can become content with their accomplishments and cease to continue taking the necessary action to grow and improve.

"

The basic building block of good team building is for a leader to promote the feeling that every human being is unique and adds value
- ANONYMOUS

People feel comfortable giving when the atmosphere feels comfortable to contribute to. In teams, groups, or relationships, it will often take someone to step up to set the tone that all persons matter.

No matter what accomplishments you make, somebody helped you..

- ALTHEA GIBSON

Remember to be mindful of the words "I made it on my own" or "I did it by myself." Neither is possible. Someone supports you. Someone gives you an opportunity. Someone circulates a resource for you. It's very little that we can actually do on our own. With that said, remember that relationships matter.

Light is the task where many share the toil.

- HOMER

Life can be really difficult when we operate as solo beings. Life can seem unbearable from the heaviness. However, when others are participating in life with you, it relieves a significant amount of weight. Life becomes lighter.

T.E.A.M = Together everyone achieves more.

- ANONYMOUS

A gentle reminder, no matter the relationship, collective efforts is always more powerful than individual input.

AFFIRMATIONS

I am whole.

I am enough.

Where I am, is perfect.

I embrace who I am, and accept where I am.

I am resilient.

I am free.

I deserve joy.

Joy, goodness, and things fruitful and nurturing are available to me.

I am love.

I matter. I release any previous narratives that challenge otherwise. No one determines my value but me. I am valuable and deserving because I was blessed to be alive. That is enough, and I am enough.

I am enough, now, always and forever. I remain open to relationships and experiences that continue to reflect this truth. I release relationships, experiences, and thoughts that reflect limitations of my full self.

My strength and vulnerability are indicators of my humanness. I let others help me when I know there are difficulties in handling heavy weights. I express my emotions because they matter. I am complex. I am human. My resilience in the past provides me with the ability to keep going and not stop.

I embrace my authentic self. I am open to sharing all versions of my true self because I deserve to be seen. I know my voice and perspective matter. I am proud to take up space.

I am loveable. I have examples all around me to affirm my value in the world. I will continue to embrace who I am and give up the desire to find validation of my worth in others.

I am a magnet for healthy relationships.

I am capable of igniting change around me.

I am covered by peace, comfort, and protection.

I act on opportunities that will elevate me to my next level.

I am aware of yet not overcome by my fears.

I accept the complexity of my being. I will work to always grow but release the idea that I need to fix myself. I am a collection of experiences, but my experiences do not define me. I am a reflection of my family, but I embrace my individuality. I am not defined by the judgements and opinions of others.

I am loved. I am supported. I am nurtured. I am cared for.

I can make this world a better place. I will share who I am, and my gifts to contribute to the world around me. My talents, skills, and gifts matter.

I have everything that I need. I am exactly where I am supposed to be to receive what is for me to take into my next season. I practice gratitude in order to ground myself and bring forth more resources.

I am more than my body. I am a being full of hopes, dreams, desires, hobbies, emotions, and opinions. I will embrace my full self, and release fixation on my outer appearance as the sole indicator of who I am.

I am worthy of love. I release ideas that I am not enough or deserving of receiving healthy, nurturing, and reciprocal love.

My mind is focused on abundance of all forms.

I release the desire to fix myself because I am enough. I have nothing to prove. I am unique and embrace who I am.

I am exactly where I need to be. I release any critical thoughts or beliefs about my current place in life. I am receiving what I need at this moment. I am grateful for the experiences and knowledge I have collected. I am at peace.

I am loved. I am loveable. I am worthy of love. I am love.

I embrace the challenges presented to me with gratitude. I look for the lessons available to me. I am constantly growing.

I am doing my best. I acknowledge that my best looks different from moment to moment and will be gentle with myself for wherever I am at this moment is perfect.

I create relationships built on reciprocity.

I forgive myself. I did the best that I could do, and now that I know more, I will make decisions from a place of intention and higher consciousness.

I feel love, joy, abundance, and peace.

Abundance is available to me.

I bring value into the world.

I let go of all that does not serve me.

I am committed to investing in, nurturing, and contributing to healthy relationships.

I am surrounded by love in many forms. I take gratitude in the people that love and accept me. I make sure to extend to others the compassion, kindness, and grace that I seek.

Abundance is my birthright.

I am overflowing with ideas that will bring prosperity.

I am healed. I am whole.

I am in control of my reactions. I interact with the world around me from a place of intended response and not impulsive reaction. I am intentional with how I express myself.

My body is healthy.

I allow the flow of abundance and prosperity in my life.

I am powerful.

I am resilient.

I am open to receiving support and care from others.

I trust that my life is unfolding in a way that serves my highest good.

I embrace my ability to choose healthy relationships and environments that allow me to thrive.

I am full of all the possibilities that I envision.

The abundance I seek is available and constantly seeking me.

My ability to conquer my challenges is limitless.

I pursue the day with strength in my heart and clarity in my mind.

I operate through love and not fear.

I am grateful for my freedom. I am grateful for my life experiences.

I welcome positive life experiences and relationships in my life.

I move with love, confidence, and courage.

I love myself. I embrace all my complexities. I accept all of me
with compassion and honor.

I am courageous.

I use fear to propel me. I challenge myself to move thru what
fears me with strength and faith. I am more than a conqueror.

I pursue each day with the intention to do my best, give my best, make a difference, and experience pleasure.

My value is not determined by someone else's willingness to love and accept me.

I am more than my pain and loss.

There is a strength within me that allows me to continue moving through life with hope.

My vulnerability and ability to share myself is a gift and act of courage.

There is light in the darkness I have experienced. My story is a gift of healing and renewal for another.

My power lies in my authenticity.

My heart is expansive and has the capability to love and be
loved.

I take care of all that and who that matters to me.

I am blessed.

I am infinite. I am multidimensional. I am everything that has shaped me. I am everything that I long to be.

I have the power to evolve. I can release stories and old versions of myself that are no longer aligned with the life I want.

I am not limited to being who I once was. I have the power to embrace a new version of myself.

I am allowed to change my mind about the person I want to be and the life I want to live.

Life offers me the opportunity to choose every day. I am intentional with the choices that I make. I am intentional about my life.

I have the capacity to be both a teacher and a student. I embrace the people, relationships, opportunities, and experiences that feed me knowledge. I surrender to the relationships and opportunities I have to be of value to someone else.

I am proud of every version of myself. They have led me to this very moment of consciousness and enlightenment.

I celebrate the ways that I love myself because this world makes it challenging to do so.

I am grateful for the steps I have taken towards wholeness. I stay in constant pursuit of wholeness.

I am worthy to receive.

I live every day with intention. I make decisions that lead me to a destination of fulfillment and contentment.

Peace and ease are available to me.

I focus on my peace.

I am ready to receive all that I desire.

I am committed to cultivating joy daily.

I am open to creating healthy, safe and supportive spaces for others.

I take responsibility for my healing and journey to higher consciousness.

I release the responsibility of my happiness being controlled, determined, or created by others.

I do good to others and help improve the state of the world.

I honor other people's boundaries.

I embrace and respect other people's differences.

I am an active participant in all relationships and release the blaming of others.

I take steps to repair and nurture relationships that are significant to me.

I do my best to show up as my best in all of my relationships.

I am honest.

I am a blessing to this world.

I choose to maintain my groundedness despite the chaos that surrounds me.

I have the power to choose how I respond to my environment. I choose the form of expression that honors my voice, my value, and my peace.

I do the best that I can every day.

I approach every day knowing that I can forge a new path and make informed decisions that lead me to where I want to be.

I take the steps that I need to empower myself every day.

I am proactive about taking the necessary steps to motivate myself every day.

I honor my full self.

I honor my body.

I honor my mind.

I honor my spirit.

I practice forgiving myself and others daily.

www.ingramcontent.com/pod-product-compliance
Lightning Source LLC
Chambersburg PA
CBHW010939140726
47988CB00010B/3519